REAL MEN ARE SEXIER WHEN THEY ARE TRANSPARENT

Compiled by Pastor Troy R. Jones.
Featuring Donovan Griffin, Victor Major, Lawrence
Martin, Stephen Walwyn

ISBN: 9798884119659

Printed in the United States of America.

DEDICATION

To all the men who have embraced vulnerability and authenticity, defying societal norms and expectations. Your courage to be transparent and true to yourselves is not only commendable but also undeniably sexy. May this book serve as a celebration of your strength and an inspiration to others. Thank you for being a shining example of what it means to be a man of transparency and authenticity.

Table of Contents

FOREWORD

By Dr. Tamiko Lowry

I t is with great pleasure and admiration that I write this foreword for "Real Men are Sexier When They are Transparent" by Pastor Troy R. Jones. This book marks the beginning of a profound journey, one that delves into the depths of manhood, transparency, and the intricate layers of masculinity.

Through the compelling narratives of five diverse authors, this book unveils the complexities, challenges, and triumphs encountered on the path to authenticity and vulnerability. Pastor Troy R. Jones, Donovan Griffin, Victor Major, Lawrence Martin, and Stephen Walwyn come together to share their stories, offering insights, reflections, and revelations that resonate with readers from all walks of life.

These narratives serve as beacons of hope, courage, and resilience, inviting readers to embark on a transformative exploration of self-discovery and growth. In a world that often pressures men to conform to societal expectations, these authors bravely challenge the norms and share their personal experiences to inspire others.

"Real Men are Sexier When They are Transparent" sheds light on critical issues facing men today. The statistics reveal the staggering prevalence of abuse, neglect, and societal challenges encountered by men. It is disheartening to learn that 24 percent of domestic violence survivors are men. These statistics underscore the urgency of fostering open dialogue, dismantling stigma, and fostering support systems for men navigating through adversity.

I am particularly inspired by the work of 108 Community Organization, spearheaded by Troy R. Jones. The organization's commitment to providing resources, advocacy, and empowerment for men and their families is commendable. The weekly men's support group provides a safe space for individuals to share experiences, seek guidance, and cultivate resilience. This initiative fosters a sense of community, understanding, and healing.

"Real Men are Sexier When They are Transparent" is more than just a collection of stories; it is a call to action, an invitation to engage in meaningful dialogue, and a testament to the transformative power of transparency and vulnerability.

Let us remember that no instance of domestic violence is justified, and whether you're male or female, it's never your fault. Together, let's break the silence, shatter stigma, and pave the way for a future where transparency, compassion, and understanding thrive.

Dr. Tamiko Lowry

Trauma Recovery Coach & Domestic Violence Expert

PREFACE

In today's fast-paced and ever-evolving world, the concept of masculinity has undergone a profound transformation. Traditional notions of strength, stoicism, and invulnerability are increasingly giving way to a more inclusive and authentic understanding of what it means to be a man. As we navigate this paradigm shift, it becomes imperative to explore and redefine the role of transparency in men's lives and relationships.

In this co-authored masterpiece, "Real Men are Sexier When they're Transparent," I am honored to present the collective voices of extraordinary individuals who have embarked on a journey of self-discovery, vulnerability, and personal growth. Together, we delve into the depths of our individual experiences, shining a light on the transformative power of transparency.

Throughout these pages, you will encounter candid narratives that invite you to walk alongside us on our paths to adulthood and intimate relationships. We share our triumphs, our struggles, and the lessons we have learned along the way. By peeling back the layers of societal expectations and cultural conditioning, we aim to challenge prevailing stereotypes and ignite conversations that inspire positive change.

Transparency, we believe, is the key that unlocks a new world of possibilities for men. It is the catalyst that fosters authentic connections, nurtures emotional well-being, and liberates us from the shackles of outdated masculine norms. By embracing transparency, we empower ourselves to express our vulnerabilities, communicate our needs, and engage in meaningful dialogues that cultivate healthy relationships.

Within these pages, you will find stories of men who have embraced their true selves, defying societal pressures and unveiling the strength found in their authenticity. Their narratives illuminate the beauty of vulnerability and the profound impact it has on personal growth, emotional resilience, and the development of nurturing partnerships.

As you embark on this literary journey, we invite you to open your heart and mind to the possibilities that lie within each story. Let these tales serve as a catalyst for your own self-reflection and growth, encouraging you to examine the depths of your own journey and relationships. It is our collective hope that the insights shared within these pages will inspire men and women alike to celebrate transparency as a transformative force in our lives.

Together, let us embark on this transformative expedition towards redefining masculinity, embracing transparency, and fostering a world where "Real Men are Sexier When They are Transparent."

Senior Pastor Troy R. Jones Author and Co-Author of "Real Men are Sexier When they're Transparent"

WELCOME TO NOVEL NECTAR
A UNIQUE READING EXPERIENCE

"Real Men are Sexier When They are Transparent" extends a warm invitation to readers of all backgrounds on an extraordinary journey led by five courageous authors, including the visionary Pastor Troy Jones. In this collective exploration, societal norms surrounding masculinity are challenged, offering unfiltered narratives of self-discovery and relationships.

In the ever-evolving landscape of literature, innovation often sparks from the fusion of tradition and novelty. It is within this realm of exploration that we proudly introduce "Novel Nectars" to the literary world—a groundbreaking concept poised to redefine the reading experience as we know it.

Prepare to engage in Novel Nectars, a dynamic experience specifically crafted for this groundbreaking project. Each author, with their unique perspective, has chosen a beverage to accompany their chapter, adding a delightful twist to your reading adventure.

As you embark on the journey through "Real Men are Sexier When They are Transparent," we invite you to partake in a unique fusion of storytelling and sensory indulgence. With each chapter, you'll discover a carefully curated selection of beverages—aptly named "Novel Nectars"—that serve as companions to the narratives woven by our courageous authors.

Novel Nectars is more than just a title; it's an inclusive celebration inviting readers of all genders to sip, read, and savor the profound honesty, love, and redemption woven into each chapter. This literary libation affair is a toast to real men redefining sexiness through transparency and an open invitation for readers of every identity to join the celebration.

This fusion of literature and libation aims to engage your senses in ways previously unexplored. Through the subtle interplay of taste, aroma, and emotion, Novel Nectars seeks to elevate your reading experience, inviting you to immerse yourself fully in the world of each chapter.

So, whether you choose to indulge in the identified beverage that pairs perfectly with each chapter or prefer to sip on a favorite drink of your choice, Novel Nectars welcomes you. Cheers to an adventure where the authenticity of the authors meets the nuanced notes of your chosen libation, creating an experience that transcends the ordinary and welcomes all to the journey of self-discovery and love.

And remember, should time or circumstance prevent you from enjoying each beverage alongside its corresponding chapter, fear not. You can always return to savor the unique flavor of each narrative, experiencing the richness of transparency at your own pace.

Pastor Troy R. Jones

Troy R. Jones, a Pastor, certified life coach, and international speaker, has become a transformative force in the lives of many. As a five-time author and social advocate for "Healthy Masculinity," he is a resilient survivor of domestic violence, recognized as the Keynote Speaker for the Nation's Capital in 2022 and 2023 during Domestic Violence Awareness Month. His impact extends to being the Keynote Speaker for the Morgan State University Youth Summit in 2022, leading to the integration of his rites of passage program into Mt Zion Preparatory School in Prince Georges County, Maryland.

Troy is the visionary founder and president of the 108 Community Organization, a nonprofit committed to holistic healing for men and their families dealing with various forms of trauma. With over twenty-five years of experience, he has worked tirelessly to help individuals of all backgrounds discover and achieve their greatest potential. In the face of societal expectations, he emphasizes the importance of protecting and empowering both men and women, standing by males to instill resilience.

Acknowledging that 1 in 6 men has faced sexual assault and abuse, Troy sheds light on this silent struggle. His B6 Men's Support Group, meeting weekly since February 12, 2014, addresses trauma associated with neglect, domestic abuse, and emotional struggles. The group has grown to 350 members, a testament to its success in offering strength, compassion, and a path to recovery.

As a certified integrative mental health counselor, Troy's leadership in creating the B6 Men's Support Group has provided an invaluable space for men to recover and maintain healthy relationships. This commitment aligns with his broader mission of creating opportunities for transparent dialogues, inspiring men to seek support rather than suffer alone.

Troy's literary contributions, including "The Forbidden Journal," delve into the pervasive abuse suffered by men and offer insights into their journey to healing. His earlier works, such as "The Relentless Pursuit," "Wounds to Wisdom," and "The Chain Breaking Experience Volume 6," showcase his dedication to sharing wisdom and fostering resilience.

Currently residing in Pennsylvania with his loving wife and two children, Troy R. Jones continues to be a beacon of inspiration, using his story, wisdom, and advocacy to create stronger communities and inspire individuals to embrace life's symphony of challenges and triumphs.

Troy's pairing Novel Nectar Presents:

Novel Nectar Troy's choice to pair Menage a Trois Midnight with his chapter is a poetic convergence of flavors and narratives. Just as the wine's rich and intense blend harmonizes different elements, Troy's chapter may weave together a tapestry of emotions, experiences, and reflections.

Navel Nectar invites you to enjoy the dark fruit notes and velvety texture of Midnight to complement the depth and complexity of Troy's storytelling. The wine's characteristics, like its mocha undertones and bold blackberry flavors, might resonate with the nuanced layers of his chapter, adding an extra dimension to the reader's experience.

The choice of this wine suggests an intention to elevate the reading experience, encouraging a sensory exploration that mirrors the intricacies found within the pages of Troy's narrative. It's a thoughtful pairing, inviting readers to sip and savor the words alongside the rich nuances of Menage a Trois Midnight, creating a memorable and immersive journey for both the palate and the mind.

Whether you choose to embrace the suggested Menage a Trois Midnight or opt for a libation that aligns with your personal taste, Novel Nectar celebrates the beauty of choice. Here's to an immersive reading experience where Troy's narrative seamlessly harmonizes with the chosen libation, creating a symphony of promise, trust, and enduring commitment. Cheers to the unique and resonant journey that awaits you!"

"

For I know the plans I have for you," declares the Lord, "plans to prosper you and not to harm you, plans to give you hope and a future. - **Jeremiah 29:11**

CHAPTER 1

HE KEPT HIS PROMISE

By Pastor Troy R. Jones

In the heart of Baltimore City, amid the ever-persistent city buzz, I embarked on a life-transforming journey—a life filled with faith, redemption, and a melody that almost faded into obscurity. This tale is more than just a narrative; it's an authentic story of survival, serving as a reminder that anyone, at any given moment, could find themselves teetering on the brink of existence.

Growing up in Baltimore, my introduction to the Bible at a young age was more than just a casual acquaintance. I carried one from age 4 to about 9, which, in hindsight, wasn't exactly a trendsetter's move. Nevertheless, as I matured, a specific set of verses from Titus, found in verses 1:6-9, reshaped my perspective on life. These verses became my moral compass, offering guidance akin to a GPS, steering me through life's tempests. They encapsulated a code of conduct, a set of values I embraced unwaveringly, regardless of life's trials. These scriptures laid out qualities expected of an elder, someone akin to leading a family. Though not ready for that responsibility, I believed I could start practicing those virtues.

"This biblical passage outlined an elder's attributes—blameless, faithful to one's partner, and raising well-behaved children. It described an overseer as someone managing God's household, embodying qualities of integrity, devoid of aggression, temperance, or greed. Instead, this individual should be hospitable, cherish goodness, exhibit self-control, integrity, holiness, and discipline. These principles emphasized adhering to a trustworthy message, uplifting others through sound doctrine, and challenging opposition with grace. This guidance was unlike anything I'd heard; it challenged me at my core, quietly daring me to seek it and find it amidst the conflicting voices encouraging a different path. Challenge accepted!

Baltimore's bustling environment served as the crucible for cultivating these virtues. It felt like navigating a whirlwind to seek a missing puzzle piece—a challenging task, to say the least. My youthful aspirations often clashed with my desire to embody the virtues outlined in Titus. Peer pressure and the allure of conformity stood as constant adversaries to this pursuit. In the midst of such challenges, I consciously withdrew, seeking solitude to reinforce my overarching goal.

I devoted time to introspection, tuning into my inner voice, deciphering life's enigmatic messages of morality. This journey wasn't solely about self-improvement but also about fortifying my connection with myself and a higher power, a lifeline anchoring me in life's darkest moments.

My life philosophy revolved around a simple trio: kindness, self-awareness, and mastering the art of setting boundaries. In a world that often felt like a jumbled symphony, these principles became my guiding notes, harmonizing my journey through life's highs and lows.

Amidst the ceaseless hustle of the city, a defining moment arrived when I was just fifteen. I recall strolling with my uncle and encountering an extraordinarily confident woman. Her allure was magnetic, captivating my attention entirely. I anticipated my uncle to share my fascination, yet he remained unfazed. "Aren't you going to look at her?" I inquired. His response was unexpected but profound: "No, and you shouldn't either. Let her turn and look at you because you're just as FINE as she is!" Those words became a shot of confidence, rescuing me from a lifetime of self-doubt and reinforcing the character trait I would need indefinitely "Self-Control".

In the rhythm of life, I stumbled upon a poignant realization—a truth that echoed in the corridors of my journey. It became clear that while I was earnestly working on bettering myself, the world around me didn't always echo that sentiment. Not everyone shared the same eagerness or readiness to embark on a journey of self-improvement. It was a lesson that unfolded gradually, challenging the very fabric of my being.

This understanding, raw and unfiltered, breathed life into the morals and values I held dear. In a world where the pursuit of self-improvement can often feel like a solo dance, these principles became my anchor. They weren't just lofty ideals; they were the threads that wove through the tapestry of my experiences, providing both guidance and solace. As I share this part of my journey, it's not merely a recollection but an invitation to connect, to resonate with the trials of self-discovery in a world where not everyone shares the same commitment to personal growth.

What shaped my thoughts on relationships/marriage? The earliest cornerstone in this narrative traces back to my mother's marriage, a chapter that began with an idyllic vision of family. In those formative years, my father stood as a figure of vigor in my life, his presence embodying my understanding of what a strong familial bond should resemble. However, life has a way of unfolding unexpected twists. The trajectory of our family story shifted dramatically as he grappled with the clutches of addiction. His choices led our once-healthy family dynamic to fracture, leaving me grappling not only with the dissolution of their marriage but also with a revelation that shook the very foundations of my identity. In the midst of the chaos, it was revealed to me with a startling clarity—I wasn't biologically related to the man I had called Dad. He was, in fact, my stepfather."

Following the divorce, the adults in my life moved forward, replacing each other with new partners. Yet, for me, there wasn't a man who stepped into the role of a loving and nurturing father figure. My biological father lived miles away, raising his own family, and my stepfather, no longer bound by marriage, was no longer obligated to me. While both sets of my siblings had paternal figures in their lives, I lacked that presence. I found myself without a male role model, without someone to emulate or connect with on a paternal level.

The men in my vicinity seemed to wear the titles of womanizers, thugs, hustlers, or a blend of all three with a twisted sense of pride. To them, this was just how life worked, and questioning their lifestyle was an unheard-of notion. Amidst these influences, I stood my ground, acutely aware of the moral compass within me. Even in the absence of a guiding paternal figure, I refused to align myself with their choices.

As I looked around, I found solace in the glowing screens of television, where family sitcoms became my surrogate kin. These shows depicted a stark contrast to the reality I knew— an idealized portrayal of men coming home to a warm and loving family, engaging in genuine laughter, displaying affection, and imparting discipline without a trace of abuse or neglect. It was a depiction that seemed to resonate with a sincere desire to be present for their children. This televised image stirred a longing within me—an earnest desire for a family life that, though distant, became an aspiration etched in the core of my being.

Understanding the slim likelihood of experiencing such familial warmth during my childhood, I made a deliberate choice to aspire to become the nurturing husband and father I had yearned for in my own future. My commitment was to break the cycle, providing the love and comfort I had missed to my own children someday.

From as early as I could recall, the desire to be married had always burned within me. I held onto that wish so fervently that I once mentioned to my mother that I was open to an arranged marriage. After all, who knew me better than her? However, my eagerness for marriage seemed to affect my dating life negatively. I apparently exuded a "spouse vibe" when what most of the women I encountered sought was a "short-term, let's-have-fun-for-now" vibe. It was a tough balancing act.

"One night in a lively Baltimore nightclub, my eyes locked onto a captivating young lady surrounded by her friends. Encouraged by the cheers of my friends, I summoned the courage to approach her. In my mind, I confidently thought, 'I've got this!' Following the rehearsed moves my mother and I had practiced over the years, I extended my hand and asked her for a dance. For a brief moment, time stood still—I felt invincible. However, that fleeting confidence was shattered as she burst into laughter, mocking me openly. 'Man, get the hell out of my face with your corny ass!' she sneered. The humiliation echoed as I walked back across the floor, sensing the weight of every eye fixed on me.

Immediately after this incident, a guy with an air of arrogance approached her, uninvitedly grabbed her hand, and whisked her onto the dance floor. To my surprise, she seemed to enjoy it. That night became a pivotal moment for me. I realized the need to navigate a delicate balance between the naturally good guy I was and the bad boy persona that appeared to attract women. It was a frustrating dilemma—I just wanted to be authentic, yet the fear of loneliness loomed large. There's nothing worse than being the guy who leaves the place without the girl.

Reflecting on that night, I often wondered if the presence of a loving father might have provided different advice, altering the course of subsequent events. The memory of my uncle's words, 'you are just as fine,' played like a soothing melody in my mind, transforming my approach. I vowed never to face rejection like that again, finding a newfound resilience that reshaped my journey in the realm of relationships.

The answer to whether societal or cultural pressures shaped my perspective on relationships is a nuanced yes and no. Society projected an image of relationships that didn't align with my desires—a prevalent promotion of a 'Playboy' lifestyle, where men were expected to engage with multiple women without consequences, using money and sex as the main currency to keep women in a certain place. Sadly, this perspective confronted me in reality, contradicting my own beliefs.

After that turning point in the nightclub, I was never again intimidated to approach a woman; in fact, the opposite became true. Many women seemed reluctant to engage with me. If my confidence captivated them, my values often pushed them away. Despite genuinely wanting to understand a woman—her thoughts, dreams, goals, hobbies—before anything physical, my approach often led to negative reactions. Even if she was considered stunning by societal standards, expressing a desire for a deeper connection resulted in her feeling upset, rejected, questioning my sexuality, and storming off, telling me to never contact her again. It was baffling because I was simply showing restraint and respect for both of us. Just because I was bettering myself didn't mean others did the same. Society painted women as fine jewels worthy of opening doors, placing coats over puddles, and getting to know them as humans, not just objects of desire. Needless to say, these reactions to kindness, restraint, and respect played tricks on my mind. Nevertheless, I held firm to my values, refusing to conform.

In the intricate chapters of my past marriage, a tale unfolded—a story etched with pain, betrayal, and the bewildering echoes of confusion. It was a journey where understanding and open-mindedness gradually morphed into fragments of trust, each revelation cutting through the delicate fabric of our union.

The descent into darkness began innocently enough. My wife, fueled by a desire to reclaim missed opportunities from her previous marriage, expressed a wish to visit a strip club. Wanting to support her growth, I agreed, thinking plans with her mom and sisters would be harmless—a chance to bridge the gaps in our rocky relationship. Little did I know, what seemed harmless would lead to a labyrinth of lies and deceit.

As nights grew longer, suspicions gnawed at my sanity. Casual discussions at the bar morphed into secret post-strip club adventures. The truth unraveled in a raw conversation with her sister—one that shattered my trust like a tidal wave crashing over me. "I never stay past 2 am," she confessed. The lies, the cover stories involving her family—it all shattered my trust, making me question why I stayed when our family, our children, and our relationship weren't her priorities.

It wasn't just the strip club; a flood of other concerns inundated my mind—the late-night phone calls, the hidden phone, the panic if left in the open. A sickening feeling churned in my stomach.

Sharing my concerns with her sister-in-law only deepened the despair. Recalling instances where she urged me to leave work early so she could go to the club, leaving me to care for our children despite working three jobs—it was a sacrifice I felt was worth making. However, a red flag emerged that I chose to ignore—the sharp reaction to my plans for her birthday. Wanting to take her on a well-deserved date, she became distressed, suggesting I stay at work, claiming financial constraints while hiding other intentions.

Her betrayal cut deeper, perhaps because, deep down, I had hoped my suspicions were wrong. The confrontation the next day, shielded from the children's eyes, turned into a chaotic storm. I shared my knowledge about the bar, hoping for discussion, but she lashed out, blaming me for her actions. Chaos ensued—stomping, yelling, slamming objects, self-questioning answers.

Frustration and anger surged within me, and in a moment of despair, I threw my sweater on the bed—an act that inadvertently frightened her, painting her as the victim. In her distress, she locked herself in the bathroom, accusing me of attempting to harm her. The absurdity overwhelmed me.

Accused of violence for tossing a soft sweater in frustration, I questioned my sanity.

Realization dawned—I couldn't endure this anymore. Despite my love and unwavering dedication, I hadn't deserved this. I had stood by her dreams, even when they transformed into nightmares. Yet, she never acknowledged my efforts or the sacrifices I made for our family's sake. I thought it meant something, but the wreckage of our relationship spoke a different truth.

Amidst the shattered remnants of infidelity and abuse in my first marriage, a harsh reality struck—a call from another man's wife, unraveling my wife's unfaithfulness. It was the final blow in a turbulent journey. Despite my relentless efforts, the toxicity became unbearable for both me and our children. Yet, even in the aftermath of that tumultuous chapter, and despite the divorce, I fiercely clung to my belief in marriage as a sacred union established by God.

In the wake of late-night club outings and the heart-wrenching revelation of betrayal, I discovered that I had lost a significant part of myself along the way. Sacrificing oneself for another shouldn't form the foundation of a relationship. I initiated a support group, B6, to empower men seeking healthy relationships, both personally and professionally.

Over several years, I painstakingly began piecing my life back together. Resuming my lifelong passion for martial arts played a pivotal role in my journey of self-discovery. It was during one of the classes that I encountered a remarkable woman. Her refusal to complete an exercise due to discomfort, a display of authenticity I'd rarely witnessed, caught my attention. Our connection deepened during a sparring session when she landed a solid punch to my nose, yet her immediate concern for me revealed a compassion that resonated deeply.

Our first date marked a divine confirmation. After a delightful evening and a stroll through Baltimore's historic streets in Hampton, we returned to my car. Opening her car door, a small gesture, was well received. All seemed perfect until my car failed to start, triggering a wave of panic and past traumas. In that moment, she reached over, touched my hand, and her reassuring touch and calming words dissolved my fears. It was as if God spoke through her, guiding me to let Him choose.

Two years later, she accepted my proposal, and after a few years of marriage, we've been blessed with two beautiful children. Her continuous love and respect humble me every day. Through her, I realized the truth: marriage is perfect despite the flaws of the husband and wife. When two souls commit to surrender their imperfections to God and accept each other as human, the union becomes a haven of perfection. God honored my faith, mending my wounded heart, for which I am eternally grateful.

The hardest worldly thing or concept for me was to let go-completely trust God and To Love thy neighbor as you love yourself.

"My mother's wisdom reverberated through my life:

In the intricate tapestry of life's lessons, a resounding chord echoes with both challenge and grace: trust. Believing in oneself is crucial, but trusting God completely is imperative. It's an elusive art, a discipline weaving through the very fabric of existence.

Guided by my mother's teachings, I embraced a philosophy that kindness wasn't merely a gesture but an essence to be embodied—an obligation to God and a testament to my masculinity. A defining moment etched itself into my journey when I encountered a homeless woman amidst the city's bustle. Many walked past her without a second glance, but as I drew close, her weary eyes spoke volumes. In a silent dialogue, we connected on a soul-to-soul level. I offered flowers and a heartfelt message, and in that fleeting exchange, her eyes lit up with gratitude—an echo of kindness reaching the forgotten corners of human hearts.

If there's a message I wish to impart, a beacon guiding through life's labyrinth, it's encapsulated in the verses of

Matthew 7:7—"Ask, and it shall be given you; seek, and ye shall find." This scripture became my compass in Baltimore's labyrinthine streets, a testament to the unyielding power of faith to move mountains. It's an assurance that life's answers often rest in the least expected places, hidden within the folds of the everyday, waiting to be discovered by those who seek with open hearts.

Baltimore, the heartbeat of my narrative, resonates with a symphony of resilience. It's more than just a city; it's a tapestry woven with threads of hope and perseverance. In its alleyways and towering structures, I found myself amidst trials and triumphs. Here, my story sings—a ballad of survival and revival—a reminder that even in the darkest hour, the light flickers, guiding us back from the abyss.

Life's greatest masterpiece is composed amidst dissonance— the stark contrasts, the discordant notes, merging into a melody that's uniquely ours. It's a call to embrace the symphony of life, to find beauty in the cacophony, and to recognize that our deepest scars often birth our most profound songs.

Donovan Griffin

Meet Donovan Griffin, a proud native of the Bronx, whose story is a captivating blend of urban energy, academic ambition, and a commitment to shaping the future. Born and raised in the vibrant streets of the South Bronx, Donovan's journey unfolds against a backdrop that resonates with the authenticity and dynamism found in communities across the nation.

Leaving the Bronx for a momentous chapter in his life, Donovan pursued higher education at Canisius University in Buffalo, NY, graduating with a Bachelor's degree in Communications. Now, his story takes an exciting turn as he immerses himself in the MALS (Master of Arts in Liberal Studies) program at Lehman College, specializing in Urban Education. With his graduation slated for May 2024, Donovan is on the brink of an exciting new phase in his narrative.

With over a decade in education, Donovan is more than a guide; he's a catalyst for academic success. His impact extends beyond the classroom, where he has been instrumental in advising students toward Associate's and Bachelor's degrees. Furthermore, Donovan takes on a leadership role in men's programs through non-profit organizations like Harlem Children's Zone and BronxWorks, creating safe spaces and mentorship programs aimed at bolstering graduation rates and fostering leadership.

Donovan's story is an intriguing exploration of urban roots, academic pursuit, and a commitment to community—a narrative that effortlessly resonates with the heart of diverse communities nationwide. Join him on a journey that transcends boroughs and speaks to the shared dreams and aspirations found in neighborhoods across America.

Donovan's pairing Novel Nectar Presents:
"Before I Say I Do" & Rum Punch

Embark on Donovan's soul-stirring chapter, "Before I Say I Do," a narrative woven with the intricate threads of love and the profound lessons learned along the way. As you immerse yourself in the pages, allow the intimate reflections on relationships to blend seamlessly with the tropical vibes of a Rum Punch—Donovan's personal favorite libation.

Picture the dance of flavors mirroring the dance of emotions within his story. Each sip of Rum Punch becomes a companion to the wisdom Donovan imparts, a delightful counterpart to the highs and lows of love's journey. Let the warmth of the rum and the sweetness of the punch parallel the tender moments and heartfelt insights shared in his chapter.

So, grab a glass, settle in, and let the symphony of Donovan's lessons and the Caribbean-inspired Rum Punch transport you to a space where love's complexities are both celebrated and savored. Cheers to love, lessons, and the perfect pairing of literature and libation!

"

You can't have a million-dollar dream with a minimum wage work ethic.

CHAPTER 2

BEFORE I SAY I DO

By Donovan Griffin

On July 4, 2019, America's "INDEPENDENCE DAY" of ALL days, I was getting married. It was my wedding day - a once-in-a-lifetime event I have wanted and envisioned since childhood. On this day, nothing was going as planned. I rushed to put everything together to ensure it was the best day of our lives. Through all this, I realized that 1) I did not have my suit jacket or a tie, 2) I did not have the wedding ring with me, and, worst of all, 3) I hardly knew my bride's name. Forget the fact that my wardrobe was incomplete or that I did not have the ring. How the hell did I spend time in a relationship with someone whose name was a challenge to pronounce and remember!?! I hardly knew her! As I rushed back to my hotel room to get my jacket, I paused and called my bride to share major concerns. As much as I wanted to be a husband, I realized I was not ready to make a lifelong commitment to someone who was basically a stranger. Why was I trying to speed up my timeline as if I had 24 hours to live? I simply told her, "I am not where I want to be in my life." Then, I woke up. I woke up from my sleep. It was a dream with an unbelievable amount of irony and symbolism. I sighed in relief afterward. I fully understand that in a marriage, you build with your partner, make sacrifices, and face the world as an unbreakable unit that can withstand anything life throws. I still have work to do. However, I must further my transparency and vulnerability to self-reflect and acknowledge my personal growth before I become someone's husband.

As a dark-skinned Black male born and raised in the South Bronx, it was an internal battle learning to embrace my complexion as a child and early teen. My parents loved me unconditionally; however, I wanted acceptance beyond my home. Representation matters when you are a child watching TV; hardly any stars with my complexion are considered sexy and attractive. I did not feel that I was physically appealing to the girls growing up. Girls rejected me as early as kindergarten, and I carried that shame for years. Lighter-skinned guys at my schools who looked like Ricky Martin and Ginuwine got the attention. Front cover magazine models, if you will. Unless I was on a sports team and demonstrating Michael Jordan skills on the basketball court, I would not be pursued. History and media show that dark-skinned males are most valued when playing sports. I was not that guy. I followed the rules, excelled in school, and stayed lowkey. Teachers referred to me as the ideal student that others should follow, and my peers often resented me, which made me a target. My complexion was the root of the jokes, and I was not always confrontational. I was a nerd and an "African booty scratcher." If you were called an "African booty scratcher," you were likely considered ugly by many of your peers. I felt ugly among my peers, and the teasing further cemented my low self-esteem. What could I showcase beyond my stellar grades? I internalized many traumatic events because my feelings were often dismissed when expressing them. Furthermore, my transparency in school led to arguments and fights. Winning fights in school was certainly a confidence boost for me. I easily passed the test in defending myself physically; however, I failed at defending myself emotionally. Being gaslighted most times eventually silenced me. Those insecurities hindered my future relationships and dating experiences as I got older.

I always participated in class and gave the answers with ease. I was president of many clubs and organizations like Student Government in high school and CCTV (Canisius College Television) when I attended Canisius for my Bachelor's degree. I used my voice to execute plans. I had a platform to be recognized by my peers as a powerhouse. My teachers, many faculty, and staff endorsed me as I always led my teams to great success. I had the ability to self-advocate for everything other than my feelings and the personal relationships I had.

I was always convinced that I was overreacting when expressing my feelings and that I should not feel the way I did, even from my mother. My love for my mother has never been up for debate; however, I did not have a voice. Being frustrated about how she treated me was always met with a counterargument where she would remind me of the sacrifices she made to be a young parent at 19 years old. I felt like the villain and was wrong for having feelings about how she would make me uncomfortable. I would get upset when she would gossip about me to family members. "Why you got an attitude?" she said. I would share my discomfort which resulted in an argument between us. This exchange overwhelmed my mind, body, and spirit. I was tense. I did not have permission to be in my feelings. If I was really triggered, it turned into a shouting match, further escalating the tension in my body. Plus, when a parent says, "If you don't like it, you can get the fuck out!" you likely don't challenge it. Eventually, I kept my thoughts to myself. My theory was to stay silent to keep the peace. After all, she exhausted all efforts to ensure my brother and I had our basic needs met and more. The least I can do is keep my mouth shut. That is what I rationalized. I watched my father be as peaceful and non-confrontational with my mother as possible. She would raise her voice in their arguments, and he would not match her energy. If I did not express my thoughts to my mother, I would not expose myself to another verbal beatdown and feel shitty afterward. That 'staying silent theory' was ineffective for my romantic relationships early on.

The beginning of every relationship is great. It is basically the honeymoon phase. If you were like me, you want to be around them all the time; the phone calls and texts are ongoing, and it appears that the relationship will last for a long time. I agree with Janet Jackson - it is funny how time flies when you are having fun! But there were red flags that I tended to ignore. My first relationship had plenty of red flags that should have been addressed; however, I did not address them. I anticipated that exposing those flags would likely result in arguments, and there were lots to say in that first relationship that triggered me, such as her staying in contact with an ex and having inappropriate communication with him. However, I stayed silent to "keep the peace" between us. That did not work, and the relationship shattered after four months. I partially contributed to the downfall of that relationship because I was not transparent when I should have been. I sacrificed my feelings to try to have a long-lasting relationship with someone I thought was worthwhile and as invested in making it work as I was. However, I was wrong and felt deflated.

You would think I learned my lesson about expressing my emotions for the next relationship I would be in five years later. I did not. I was still guarded with my feelings and afraid to be vulnerable. A month after our relationship started, I was fired from my first salary-paying job at BronxWorks. How would I take the lead in a new relationship if I did not have an income? After all, I am a man who is supposed to have financial stability, right? She offered openness and compassion, and I worked tirelessly to secure employment. However, I was dishonest about my inner feelings. She recognized the signs I displayed through my silence and demeanor, yet I would dismiss them. I worked harder to convince her that everything was OK than to admit I was not. One evening after our date, we were on the train heading to our homes and had a conversation I was bothered by. I cannot recall the specifics of it, but I recall her saying something that disturbed me. I became quiet for the rest of the train ride, and she inquired about my feelings. "What's wrong?" she asked. My default response to that and many other times when people asked was, "Nothing. I'm good." That response was a cover-up because my inner child expected people to say I was too sensitive.

This was the first time in my dating experience that someone inquired about my feelings and was willing to investigate with me. I could see my girlfriend's sincerity. But rather than share the details of my feelings while in her company, I waited until we were on the phone later that evening to express myself. She was annoyed and expressed disappointment. Our conversation that night ended abruptly, and she ignored my calls and texts for the next 24 hours. I finally had the bravery to be vulnerable but felt I was being punished for it. The word 'disappointment' is a trigger word for me. It is one of the most uncomfortable feelings to have. To know that I let someone close to me down through my actions when I had an opportunity to prevent it felt like the world was over. I sat in guilt, shame, and discomfort for that period, anticipating that she would break up with me soon after.

She finally returned my calls, and I apologized for withholding my emotions while sharing the norm I created by internalizing negative feelings. Outside of my small circle of friends, who could I refer to within reach to have an outlet for expressing my feelings openly and for them to be acknowledged without criticism? I was guarded, and my experiences with my mother always made me feel that the details I shared about my feelings would be used as ammunition to fire back at me when things were bad between us. My family did not create space to share our feelings or encourage them, and I recognized that many of them grew up in settings where it was not encouraged either. It is not likely for older family members, especially parents, to replicate a positive practice if they did not experience it themselves. Imagine crying your eyes out as a child, and your mother says to you, "STOP CRYING BEFORE I GIVE YOU SOMETHING TO CRY ABOUT!" There was no comfort there. Between my parents, she was the disciplinary figure for our family while my father was the provider. I love them dearly but I confided more with my closest friends.

Most of my closest friends are women I spent years building and reciprocating trust with before I could be fully transparent. My girlfriend was concerned that I was more expressive with them than her. I can understand and empathize with the irritation someone can have when they want to be there for you emotionally but watch you connect with friends instead. My friends have watched me at my lowest through my tragedies, including my father's passing during my junior year of college, my mother's near-death experience with three consecutive heart attacks during my last semester of college, and all of the anxiety and depression episodes I have had. So, it was easy to disclose raw information to them. My girlfriend and I eventually became distant, and the relationship was over after a 7-month period. Every relationship comes with a major lesson; this relationship empowered me to be more vocal and expressive when in a relationship.

So, I took another hiatus from dating and relationships for a lengthy period. I was happy spending time alone and enjoying my company. I secured employment again in

September 2014, working at Harlem Children's Zone, right before my unemployment benefits ended. My workaholic tendencies were something I owned for years. I was proud to overexert myself. Not taking care of myself all for the sake of excelling at work. I am an educator, and students' needs have always been my top priority. I felt it was necessary to be in grind mode. I was single and wanted to use my free time to build my resume and credentials in an effort to plan my future as a husband and father. I have ALWAYS wanted to have a family of my own. And years later, at 34 years old, my mental condition is far better than before. It took a fatal health crash and being diagnosed with Multiple Sclerosis in October 2016 to finally invest in my care and well-being. This prompted me to return to counseling and monthly support groups since college. These efforts empowered me to vocalize my feelings guilt-free and embrace transparency. I date with intentions to be authentic and "put everything on the table" early and frequently to prevent surprises that could be detrimental.

So... to the love of my life and future mother to our beautiful babies, BEFORE I SAY 'I DO' to you and you claim my last name, I NEED to know your first and middle name! LOL, I will NOT experience deja vu through that dream I had. My name is Donovan Devore Griffin. I am imperfect and describe myself as an extroverted-introvert. I don't know how we will meet. Maybe we have met already. I do not know, but if we are in conversation and you find that I cannot stop talking to you, I am likely comfortable in your presence, which is a major plus. Many people, particularly women, have found that I can have a serious demeanor or quiet. Don't be too alarmed. I have been told this since childhood, which can be annoying. Again, I am an extroverted introvert who always protects my peace. Many, often the same ones who assume I am "too serious," are the ones who will also share that I am funny AF and easy to talk to. I want us to ALWAYS be honest with each other. Even the most uncomfortable conversations can be the most transformative for our future together. My most recent dating experiences have set the tone for my relationship expectations. I want us to always LIVE in the moment. I want to have a relationship where we are always laughing. Not many people can get me to laugh until my stomach hurts. The woman who can do that will have my undivided attention.

And, BEFORE I SAY 'I DO,' I need to know that you will not give up on me. In today's generation, where Black men, especially dark-skinned Black men like myself, are not often acknowledged positively, always stereotyped and criminalized in the media, and killed rapidly, I cannot afford to be with anyone who does not value me to the absolute fullest! I have a long history of not giving myself grace through my efforts to succeed. There is no need to be with someone who will contribute to that stress. I need you to be patient with me as I continue elevating. I am a work in progress and am dedicated to counseling every Thursday at 8PM to work through my anxiety and other personal matters. I will generate the results I have worked hard for on my timeline. Furthermore, some did not always reciprocate the same energy and effort as I did. And I overstayed my welcome in their lives as a result. My existence is not something you just tolerate like a piece of gum on the bottom of a shoe. I refuse to settle for anything less than a two-way partnership where we are dedicated to our relationship growing and flourishing while also elevating each other to be the absolute best. I expect our marriage to have seasons of happiness, heartache, disappointments, and tragedies. However, I want longevity! I need to have full-time certainty that you will be the roots of my tree and not the leaves that fall off forever.

I am sincerely looking forward to our love story! I am thrilled for the journey of discovering who you are and meeting the important people in your life who have helped shape you into the woman with whom I want to spend eternity with. See you at the alter <3

P.S.: For our wedding, I am open to any date and month except July 4th and August...ESPECIALLY AUGUST! LOL #iykyk #noentanglementshere

Victor Major

Victor Major, a man of multifaceted experiences and unwavering dedication, draws his life's narrative against the backdrop of Alexandria, VA. Born to Eleanor and Eugene Major, Victor stands as the youngest among his siblings, which includes two older brothers, Gene and Jay, and sisters Kathy and Lynne, the latter transitioning from this realm.

Immersed in the spiritual embrace of Alfred Street Baptist Church and Roberts Memorial Methodist Church during his formative years, Victor navigated the path of education at Mt Vernon High School. His journey continued through Northern Virginia Community College and the historically black Virginia Union University in Richmond, VA, adding layers of knowledge to his evolving story.

Victor's professional journey commenced during his college days as a student aid at the Department of the Army Material Command (DARCOM), laying the foundation for a remarkable career spanning over 25 years within the Department of Defense, predominantly at the Pentagon. From a diligent mail clerk, he ascended through the ranks, becoming a classified clerk and supervisor before venturing beyond the federal government.

Currently residing in Baltimore, Maryland, Victor serves as a metro bus operator for the State of Maryland Transit Authority. His personal life is woven with love and family, having entered the bond of marriage with Arlene Major in 2016. As a proud father of five children—Marcus (biological child), and stepchildren Anton Wallis-Jones, Alexandra Jones, Daniel Wallis, and Julian Walls—Victor also embraces the joys of grandfatherhood with Ameer Kyrie and Serenity. Soon, he anticipates adding the role of father-in-law to Erica Zamora.

A born-again believer since 2007, Victor finds spiritual nourishment at Baltimore Baptist Church, where he not only attends but actively contributes as a Trustee and leader of the Men's Bible Study. Beyond his professional and familial commitments, Victor is the visionary behind the Gentlemen of Destiny (G.O.D.) mentoring program. This initiative is dedicated to nurturing young men into Kingdom Men, instilling values that resonate within the community and beyond. Victor's life is a compelling narrative, blending faith, service, and a commitment to shaping the destinies of those around.

Victor's pairing Novel Nectar Presents:

Novel Nectar, thoughtfully curated for this collaborative endeavor, invites you to savor the essence of Victor's insights while sipping on a Green Pineapple Smoothie. Allow the refreshing blend of green hues and tropical notes to complement the rich narrative and lessons shared by Victor.

Feel free to partake in the recommended Green Pineapple Smoothie or, if you prefer, select a beverage that resonates with your personal taste. Novel Nectar embraces the beauty of individual preferences. Here's to a captivating reading experience, where Victor's prose intertwines seamlessly with the chosen libation, creating a symphony of self-discovery and unconditional love. Cheers to the unique journey that awaits you!

"

> Three things will last forever – faith, hope and love and the greatest of these is love.
> **- 1 Corinthians 13:13**

CHAPTER 3

LEARNING TO LOVE UNCONDITIONALLY

By Victor Major

I was born and raised in Alexandria, VA, a small but proud and historic city just outside of Washington, DC. The youngest of five children, there are three boys and two girls. We were blessed to have two loving parents to be nurtured and raised by in our lives and household. My parents were traditional in their approach to raising children and the stature of our family. My mother was the nurturer with the soft and loving approach. She was very kind, considerate, patient, humble, caring, sweet and understanding. Mom was the type of person you could not help but to love. Everyone that would get to know her loved her immensely. Dad was the man's man. He was a strong, stern, caring, tough disciplinarian with a good heart. My father was like the the "Father" of the neighborhood.

I was fortunate to be the baby of the family and got to spend a lot of time with both of my parents. I guess they figured it was their last chance they had to get it right (lol). They both poured plenty of knowledge, wisdom and encouragement into me. It's hard to say who influenced me more growing up but I would say as a kid it was more of my father but from my late teens to early adulthood, it was my mother. My father's side of the family, meaning his brother and sister, were all accomplished. On both sides of the family, it was normal to see married couples. From the outside looking in it appeared that everyone was happily married and without strife.

I thank God that both families were God-fearing people so you know we were raised in the church. That would be the foundation for everything for me. Knowing how my parents were raised and where they came from really helped me understand who they were, why they operated the way they did in their relationship and in the raising of my siblings and myself. While my parents went through their ups and downs in their relationship. We always knew they loved each other. That was the model for me.

As a young man both of my parents shared things with me about their relationship with each other but really imparted a lot of wisdom in me about being a man and being a father. I guess that forced me to mature faster because he was always in my ear (literally lol). With all that information and observation, I knew I wanted to be a husband and father. My parents were great examples of what unconditional love is all about even though they had their share of problems in their marriage and raising a family, their love for us had no condition. I would probably describe their marriage as functionally dysfunctional but the love was never in doubt.

Having both, my parent in the household was the template for me to take into my adult life as I sought to marry and have my own family. I never really felt any real societal or cultural pressure regarding relationships. It became a natural flow because of seeing my brothers and sisters in relationships. It all felt natural.

After several failed relationships where there was no true foundation to build on, meaning there was attraction, lust, or just desire to be with someone, and no real idea of how to communicate inside of the relationship. I realize I had to take a step back to look at mistakes made, look into the mirror, spend some time removing unrealistic expectation, and realize what it was I really wanted and needed in a mate. By spending time alone, without the distractions of a relationship I came to understand through prayer, meditation, and listening to God, what I truly desired in an intimate relationship. God put in my spirit the three things I had to have in the woman I chose to marry. First, she had to be a woman who loved God, because that would have to be the foundation of our life. Second, she had to be a friend because we will have a lifetime together and who better to spend all of your time with than a friend. Third, she had to be someone who would love me unconditionally because I wanted the love to be real, unselfish and lasting. I knew these things were from God because he knows me better than I know myself and these are things that I desired to because of my relationship with him.

Fundamentally, there were things I learned over the years about relationship that I knew in my heart and mind that also had to be there to build a long and lasting marriage. Trust being one of those things because without it the devil would be busy creating havoc in our minds with all of the negative thought of what someone could be doing (imagination running wild). Nothing unhealthy grew from this but what I had gone through became part of the learning process. Learning to communicate became an importance as well as learning to remove the physical attraction and befriending someone to know who they were.

It was easy for me to learn to become friends first. I was always a big guy and the women I was attracted to didn't always feel the same way and I could not be mad because I realized that everyone you are attracted to is not meant for you. I could always learn to love them for who they are and find comfort in just being friends. That way there was no hard feelings and I could get to know them better and find out who they really are.

In my failed relationships, I neglected the friend first principle and let the attraction lead the way. I realized that this principle was my way of learning to love unconditionally.

Honesty is another bedrock characteristic because without it, it becomes so hard to build the trust that is so very necessary for making someone feel secure in his or her place in the relationship. The last and most important staple of a great relationship is communication because we have to be able to respectfully talk our way through all the issues, problems, situations and difficulties that we all go through in our life and relationships.

When my wife and I got together, I was not running from marriage or to it either but I knew that I wanted to be married. After years of being friends, something changed in how we started to see each other and I think our relationship blossomed organically. There was always an attraction but that did not dominate the feelings we had and I believe because we were friends for so long we just saw each other for who we were. There was a natural and mutual care and respect for one another. We never rushed anything in our relationship and were able to talk about everything and I believed that grew from our friendship as a foundation. When I matured enough in my spiritual life and my personal life and realized where I was and what I had, I could not ask for anything more. I had found who loved God and loved me unconditionally.

When I decided to get married, it was the best decision I made in my life. The bible says in Ecclesiastes 4:9 that two are better than one, because they have a good return for their labor. If either of them falls down, one can help the other up. That was what I wanted and needed. There are many great benefits to being married and many scriptures that guide us in marriage, but the thing that it has done for me is that it has given me a purpose and a desire to be a better man. It helped me grown, mature and become more responsible and accountable. I was recently able to share with my son and a friend of mine about how much married life has done for me. I have been pushed and challenged in ways that I could not have been while being a single uncommitted man.

Because of my submission to God and my commitment to a Christian life, God is guiding me and helping me navigate this life with a patience and humility that I know is needed to give and receive direction and correction in every area of my life.

When asked to rate my marriage, I did not have to think very long to come up with an answer. I had to say 8 or 8 1/2/. The reason it was so easy to rate it that high was because there were very few things that I see as negatives first of all but secondly there are so many positives. My wife and I have been blessed in lots of ways especially in the fact that we began our relationship as friends twenty years prior and have remained friends to this point. There were 3 things I said that

I had to have with the woman I chose to marry; 1) she had to Love God 2) she had to be a friend and 3) she had to be able to love me unconditionally. When I realized that she had these qualities, I knew I had the one for me.

As I assess the strength of my marriage, I have to look no further than the beauty of my wife and I'm not just speaking of her physical beauty, I am speaking of her inner beauty. She is such a kind and loving person with sensitivity, compassion, empathy, goodness, peacefulness and a heart that looks for the best in people Her desire to want to please is an amazing quality that I really admire in her. It makes it extremely hard for me to ever get too upset with her about anything because I believe in my heart that she always has good intentions. That does not mean that I don't want to Donkey Kong her on top of her head sometimes (doink), but it's easy to put things back in perspective.

My wife and I also try to be intentional about doing things to help our marriage grow or improve. The thing that I always try to do is look in the mirror at my actions and not just look at what I believe that she has done or not done. With us being intentional, we try to watch programs, shows, teachings and ministries that make us have discussions about where we can improve. I am sure I get on her nerves with wanting to show her different things but she is usually open to watching and listening.

Another thing we do is take time to laugh, joke and have fun with each other. We also go out and enjoy some of the things we like together such as movies, concerts, plays, jazz clubs and just being outdoors together walking or exercising. I am so delighted that we enjoy and cherish our time together. Comedy shows I think have been the most fun for us. Our desire to not be stagnant and continue to grow I believe is what is key for us.

I am so blessed to be a Christian and a child of God and to have learned what unconditional love is from the Father as well as my earthly father. There are many examples in the bible that are examples of God's love for us; (1 John 3:1 Romans 3:23, 1 John 4:7, Romans 8:37-39, 1 John 4:19, 1 Corinthians 13:4-8). These are just a few. To just know that God in his pure essence IS LOVE. To me since we are made in his image, there is only one way to walk in the real love of God in our lives and it is to learn how to draw that love from his Holy Spirit. The only way we can get his Holy Spirit to release His love into us as one of the fruits of the spirit is to be willing to enter into a true sanctification process with the Lord where He can begin the process of transforming us into the image of Christ. That is when the very love of God himself starts to flow into our personality and we can even begin to love God, love ourselves and love others to the degree or intensity that he would really desire from us. We can't try to walk in the quality of love by operating in our own strength, emotions and flesh.

Understanding and walking Gods love and grace is what I strive to do daily in my life and marriage and it is what sustains me in my most difficult times. Although I fall short of his glory, often I am still reminded by his word and conviction of his Spirit. His grace and mercy is what I try to extend because it has been extended to me and is required of me.

There have been two lessons I have learned from a couple I have resourced that have helped me tremendously. One has been the book Kingdom Man by Dr. Tony Evans. That book has really shown me what Gods design is for me as a "kingdom man", father and husband. It has truly made me look into the mirror and see my shortcomings and where I have fallen short as a man, husband and father, church member and leader in my community. I thank god for the book because it has made me stretch myself and expand my thinking about who I am as a man and my impact and influence I am to have in any community and the world (legacy).

The other resource that has impacted my thinking about my interaction in my marriage has been a service called On The Move, with Andy Stanley. In this segment he breaks down 1 Corinthians 13, particularly verse 7 where it says Love always protects, trusts, hopes and perseveres. In his main point he substitutes the word believe for trust. He touts a study about successful long-term marriage and what they all have in common, which is that they choose to believe the best about each other. In many situations in a relationship, we have what we expect and what we experience. In each between those two things, we have a choice and that is to choose to believe the worst or believe the best. He says that simple successful couples choose to believe the best about our mates in every situation.

I found that to be the best and easiest way to experience, deal with the situation with my wife because I know her heart, and choose to believe the best of her intentions always. Even when my flesh does not my spirit reminds me that her heart is pure.

I have found that the greatest obstacle to being able to love unconditionally is the flesh. God in his pure essence is Love. We are created in his image so I know we have the capacity to love this way but it is our flesh that gets in the way and how society has attached conditions on the way we love or why we love. I believe when we stop trying to love perfectly and focus on Gods perfect love, we will be able to connect with his spirit and will love his way.

Lawrence Martin

Born in the heart of Fort Wayne, Indiana, Lawrence Martin's life has been a testament to resilience and unwavering determination. At the age of 18, he faced a life-altering diagnosis of Multiple Sclerosis (MS), a challenge that could have defined him but instead became a catalyst for his extraordinary journey.

In his early twenties, Lawrence displayed entrepreneurial spirit, acquiring rental properties and laying the foundation for a future marked by business ventures. Shon's Diggity Dogs, Shon's Catering, and Lawrence Catering were the fruits of his labor, businesses that showcased his commitment to hard work and innovation.

With an associate degree under his belt, Lawrence ventured into the complexities of business ownership throughout his twenties and early thirties. However, life took an unexpected turn in his late thirties when MS manifested its most formidable challenges. Despite facing the loss of 95% of his body's functionality, Lawrence refused to surrender to despair.

Married to the love of his life for 14 years and a devoted father to two sons, Lawrence's determination knows no bounds. His dreams extend beyond personal triumphs to embody the core values he holds dear: integrity, religious convictions as a Muslim, honesty, commitment, and a fervent dedication to advocating for young black men.

In the face of physical adversity, Lawrence envisions a future where he walks independently, trains in mixed martial arts with his son, regains the freedom to drive, and, most poignantly, takes a knee to propose to his wife—a gesture MS had robbed from him.

Lawrence Martin's story is one of tenacity, love, and the pursuit of dreams against all odds. Through every trial, his spirit remains unbroken, an inspiration to those privileged to witness the resilience of a man who refuses to let circumstances define his narrative.

Lawrence's Pairing Novel Nectar Presents:

"Navigating Growth: Lessons from Life's Ups and Downs"

Embark on a transformative odyssey with co-author Lawrence in his chapter, "Navigating Growth: Lessons from Life's Ups and Downs." Within these pages, Lawrence unravels the intricacies of personal development, offering profound insights drawn from the peaks and valleys of life. As you immerse yourself in his narrative, Lawrence has chosen a Strawberry Daiquiri to accompany the journey—a vibrant and flavorful choice that echoes the richness found in the lessons shared.

Novel Nectar, exclusively tailored for this literary project, invites you to sip on a Strawberry Daiquiri as you navigate the profound wisdom woven into "Navigating Growth." Let the sweetness and zest of the daiquiri complement the sweet and poignant moments crafted by Lawrence.

Feel free to indulge in the suggested Strawberry Daiquiri or opt for a beverage of your choice. Novel Nectar celebrates individuality and preferences, ensuring that your reading experience is as unique as you are. Cheers to the harmonious blend of Lawrence's lessons and the delightful flavors that unfold with each turn of the page.

"

> *Without a struggle, there can be no progress.*
> *- Frederick Douglass*

CHAPTER 4

NAVIGATING GROWTH: LESSONS FROM LIFE'S UPS AND DOWNS

By Lawrence Marti

L et's take a moment to paint the backdrop before we delve into my story. Families, much like intricate puzzles, consist of unique pieces that contribute to the larger picture. Recent statistics tell us that single-parent households are becoming more prevalent in the United States, particularly in areas like Fort Wayne, Indiana. In this landscape, where economic challenges often intersect with personal narratives, families strive to strike a delicate balance amid the highs and lows of life.

Now, let's return to my personal narrative, a microcosm of the broader tapestry. I recount the rollercoaster of my parents' marriage, marked by occasional clashes, the sporadic presence of my father, and broken promises—a pattern not uncommon in the broader societal fabric. Visualize standing at the threshold of their bedroom, witnessing intense moments that became a tableau of our family's daily life.

My father's encounters with the legal system, marked by prison stints and shattered promises, left an indelible mark on our family's narrative. As we explore the contours of my upbringing, remember that it unfolds against a backdrop where the struggles of a single-parent household intersect with broader societal challenges. The tale that follows is one of resilience, growth, and navigating life's unpredictable twists—a story resonating not only with my own experiences but with the shared narratives of families in similar circumstances.

In one fleeting moment, hope hung in the air, pregnant with the possibility of a rekindled family bond. "I'll be back soon," he assured us. However, as the days stretched into an eternity, the optimism waned. When he finally reappeared, it was on a humble bicycle, a stark contrast to the grand promises made. In that instance, the fragility of hope revealed itself as he pedaled past our house, a poignant metaphor for the elusive stability we sought.

During his absence, my father embarked on a journey to rebuild, remarrying in pursuit of a more stable family life.

Yet, the shadows of addiction loomed large, casting a pall over these aspirations. The complexities of his struggles eclipsed the semblance of stability he sought to create. Our family narrative unfolded against the backdrop of a tumultuous quest for normalcy—a quest that remained elusive.

Amidst this tumult, my mother emerged as our unwavering rock. With Dad's presence ebbing and flowing, Mom stood as the anchor that held our familial vessel steady. The strain of maintaining equilibrium eventually exacted its toll. In 2018, three years after Dad's departure, Mom's journey on this earthly plane came to an end.

As the curtains fell on her chapter, we, her surviving kin, found ourselves thrust into the uncharted territory of a blended family. The remnants of our shattered unity lay scattered around us, waiting to be painstakingly mended. This chapter of my story, marked by the absence of a consistent paternal figure and the resilience of a mother's love, sets the stage for the transformative journey that lay ahead—my personal odyssey of growth amidst life's undulating landscape.

In the intricate tapestry of our lives, the support of our neighbors wove an indispensable thread. Among them, a particular neighbor assumed a paternal role, providing a semblance of stability. His watchful eye and caring presence became guiding lights as my brothers and I navigated the complexities of adolescence, offering solace and a sense of surrogate fatherhood during a time when we sorely needed it.

As high school beckoned, the whirlwind of teenage emotions swept me into a tumultuous relationship—one characterized by the toxic blend of jealousy and infidelity. It was a tempest that refused to abate, leading to an on-and-off cycle that seemed interminable until, inevitably, it shattered into irreparable fragments. In the aftermath, I found myself ensnared in the gravitational pull of yet another relationship, foolishly believing that this time would be different. However, the echoes of past mistakes reverberated, and history repeated itself with a haunting familiarity.

It was in the crucible of these experiences that I began to discern a vital truth—emotions, though powerful, should not be the sole navigators of life's ship. As I matured, I internalized the importance of making informed choices, steering through the tempest of emotions with a steady hand. This realization became a cornerstone of my evolving understanding of manhood—an understanding I am fervently passing on to my sons. For, in the delicate dance between vulnerability and strength, being a man is not about suppressing emotions but about wielding them wisely, ensuring they serve as allies rather than adversaries in the journey of life.

In the shadows of my past, a haunting memory lingers—a moment fueled by suspicion, a regrettable interlude that I once justified as 'normal.' In the tempest of emotions, I succumbed to a darkness that mirrored the shadows of those I had known. The embarrassment that cloaked that moment has refused to dissipate, a persistent reminder of the transient folly that can accompany unchecked emotions.

As the threads of this tumultuous chapter unfurl, it becomes evident that my gut feeling was not far off. The person in question was entangled in a romantic liaison with someone else, a revelation that cast a pall over our connection. With the revelation, she moved away, leaving behind a tapestry of unresolved emotions—a tangle of heartache and unanswered questions that would accompany me into the subsequent chapters of life.

These past experiences became poignant lessons etched into the fabric of my being. Uncontrolled emotions, much like a runaway train, can cause irreversible damage, leaving scars that endure long after the wounds have healed. This lesson, reflective of the consequences of misunderstandings in our broader community, underscores the significance of emotional intelligence in fostering understanding and cohesion.

My greatest fear, as I reflect upon this journey, extends beyond the confines of mortality. It is not merely the prospect of leaving this world but the haunting possibility of departing without the solace of inner peace. The echoes of past transgressions and the reverberations of emotional turmoil serve as a constant reminder—a clarion call to prioritize self-reflection and emotional well-being in the ongoing narrative of my life.

In the sanctuary of marriage, I've found my anchor, weathering the storms for fourteen resilient years. As the calendar pages turn, I've come to understand that maturity is not a destination reached in one's twenties, but a gradual evolution—a continuous metamorphosis shaped by the crucible of life's experiences.

Battling against the relentless tide of Multiple Sclerosis (MS), I've faced my most formidable adversary. Yet, amidst the physical and emotional tribulations, a profound truth has emerged. I've discovered that nurturing emotional well-being is not just a prerequisite for personal growth but a fundamental cornerstone for fostering enduring relationships. In the crucible of adversity, I've witnessed the transformative power of empathy, the strength derived from self-respect, and the liberating grace found in forgiveness.

The burden of clinging onto grudges is a weight that can shackle even the strongest spirit. It becomes a heavy baggage, slowing the pace of progress and hindering the journey towards personal and relational fulfillment. It's a realization born from the crucible of my own life—a truth etched into the fabric of my existence through trials and tribulations.

As I stand at the crossroads of experience, my message to the younger generation echoes through the corridors of time: emotions are fleeting, but the foundation of self-respect, empathy, and forgiveness forms.

Stephen Walwyn

In the tapestry of life, Stephen Walwyn emerges as a soul molded by the rich experiences of England, the idyllic Caribbean, and the vibrant streets of Baltimore, MD. His journey toward becoming a Family Psychotherapist at the University of Maryland felt less like a chosen profession and more like destiny and a calling.

With a spectrum of professional experiences that are both challenging and rewarding, Stephen brings a wealth of learning and humility to every opportunity that promises growth, challenge, and integration of experiences. His expertise spans human development, training, and teaching—a testament to a richly textured professional journey.

For nearly a decade, Stephen has shared his insights as an adjunct psychology professor at Washington Adventist University. Simultaneously, he has navigated the intricate realm of family therapy within various human services organizations. His role as Associate Project Director at an organization catering to individuals with intellectual and developmental disabilities showcased his commitment to diverse communities. Currently, his heart finds fulfillment as he serves veterans on a national crisis line—an expression of his profound love for service.

Rooted in the religious fervor of early childhood within Pentecostal and Seventh-day Adventist Christian denominations, Stephen's faith has evolved into a more spiritual essence. The resonance of Matthew 25 in the New Testament, urging attention to the "least of these," has become his guiding principle—an unwavering commitment to the forgotten, frustrated, and forlorn.

Stephen's narrative isn't merely a professional journey; it's a compassionate odyssey through diverse realms. From humble beginnings to a commitment to service, each chapter weaves into a tapestry prioritizing the well-being of others— a narrative in which growth, challenge, and a dedication to others take center stage.

Stephen's Novel Nectar Presents:
"ME Time VS Real Intimacy"

Join co-author Stephen on a thought-provoking journey titled "ME Time VS Real Intimacy," where he delves into the complexities of personal space and the authenticity of genuine connections. As you embark on this insightful exploration, Stephen has paired his chapter with the refreshing notes of a Green Smoothie—a choice that mirrors the vitality and rejuvenation found within the pages.

Novel Nectar, specifically curated for this project, invites you to sip on a Green Smoothie as you unravel the layers of "ME Time VS Real Intimacy." Let the crisp blend of greens and fruits complement the crisp insights and revelations shared by Stephen.

Feel free to indulge in the suggested Green Smoothie or, if you prefer, choose a beverage of your liking. The essence of Novel Nectar lies in the celebration of individuality and choice. Cheers to an enriching reading experience, where the words of Stephen harmonize with the flavors of your chosen libation, creating a symphony of self-reflection and connection.

"

> *Verily I say unto you, inasmuch as you have done it to one of the least of these my brethren, you have done it unto me.*
> *- Jesus Christ - Matthew 25:40*

CHAPTER 5

ME TIME VS REAL INTIMACY

By Stephen Walwyn

Apple News drew attention to an article in Women's Health UK magazine, highlighting the social state of the world these days. The article suggested that people are feeling a lot of "friendship anxiety" and that more people are embracing "me time" over connection. What is going on in our world, the article queries? Friendship recession is a term coined by social psychologists in the US, which means that increasingly folks are reporting that they have no close friends. Yes, spiraling costs of living forcing people to move more frequently, working longer hours and doing more side gigs in the economic and financial struggle that everyone is feeling regardless of where in the world you find yourself residing, explain [a lot of] the disconnection that everyone is feeling. There is something else going on here that is apparently worth our attention.

First of all, we have long known that social support is one of the most significant mitigating factors against the effects of stress, and a key to managing it effectively. Even more importantly, studies are now showing what many academics have long thought. When it comes to longevity and physical health, social relationships matter more than healthy weight, a good diet and regular exercise.

B6 is a men's weekly support group that addresses this basic and critical human need of meaningfully connecting with others. This group was founded and led by my friend and brother, Pastor Troy Jones. I was introduced to this group by a young lady I was dating, who clearly thought I needed what it had to offer.

She was right!

B6 is a place where men from all walks of life meet virtually. It's a space where men who've been in abusive relationships, something not talked about very much in polite society, meet up. They gather to talk about several aspects of their lives. They speak of their wounds. They motivate each other to objectively look at themselves. They attend to those aspects of themselves that led them to those toxic relationships in the first place and what might explain why they remained in them. Some of the men discover that their own behaviors in those relationships were toxic, abusive, and significantly contributed to the bad outcomes. The bloodletting, tears, and disclosures could quite easily command the attention of many Hollywood producers and writers, but for the confidentiality ethic in this very safe space. Although I didn't think so at the time I was surprised to discover I was one of those unsavory partners - a man with issues, who happened to be dating someone with her own set of issues.

I've always been fairly open with other men about my womanizing proclivities, but regrettably, not with the women that I have dated. This tendency to serially date nursed a deep seated wound caused from abandonment by well-meaning parents at an early age. What contributed even more to being a "bad boy" was my own emotional indiscipline as well as my ever present need to feed a deep longing for acceptance and gratification from women.

The one question, however, that everyone who has known me well wants to know is how can a guy who has grown up steeped in fundamentalist Christian churches, a man many regard as having some substance, and a family psychotherapist, have such struggles?

The answer to this question is not at all profound, regardless of your achievements or station in life. You could be the President of the United States or any other country for that matter. It certainly doesn't matter if you are one of the most popular preachers in the world or even if you are one of the world's best healers. The quality of the relationships that we develop with our primary caretakers will almost completely determine the quality of the relationships we develop throughout our lives, regardless of the nature of those relationships. Bolby's attachment theory along with some of the family research literature, suggests this concept throughout psychological research for over a century. Author after author conclude that during the critical stage of early childhood development - between 0-2 years of age, one either develops secure bonds of love, security, and intimacy with their parents, or one learns to distrust the world and fear attachment to others. They will instead, throughout their lifespan, likely struggle to develop appropriate and meaningful connections with those they meet in their lives. This could quite easily explain the divorce rate as being only one example of a snapshot of this dynamic.

At this early stage of infancy, many parents are anxious and preoccupied with their own unfulfilled needs from their childhood. Consequently they are unable to consistently meet the needs of their neonates in the most basic and satisfactory ways. On the other hand, there are parents, however few, who seem to get it right in raising their children at this most susceptible period of early childhood development. These parents are able to model intimacy, and demonstrate the most responsible, highly consistent attention and focus on their child's emotional needs. They have few issues of their own in fully addressing the needs of the child. When the child is wet, hungry, or just needing to be held and reassured, the child doesn't have to wait for an inordinate amount of time . The parent or surrogate, is right there with few distractions, and both consciously and unconsciously completely addresses the needs of the child. The caretaker is responsible, mature, and for the most part, have been able to sufficiently address their own personal emotional needs at some point in their life cycle.

This can happen because the parent was parented appropriately. If, however, they were not so fortunate, the best parents would have done the work for themselves. They would have sought therapy and combined self-help measures. They would also have used intentionally robust efforts to work through years of negative internal forces. Perhaps the reason why so many children suffer from abuse and neglect, is because their parents have not done the work necessary to counteract the consequences of their own parents 'rearing missteps.

Most people understand abuse and neglect. They understand them through personal experience. They learn about them through the countless stories in the media. They see it around them because of statutory bodies effecting policy and laws aimed at correcting this scourge in their respective societies.

Some parents use "neurotic" parenting simply because they have experienced this kind of parenting when they were growing up. Parents will use obsessive or compulsive parenting strategies in raising their children. They will do so as a way to subconsciously address their unfulfilled needs from their childhood. Many of these parents, often without realizing it, will have unyielding rules for their children to follow for example. They will create some rigid structure that will put a disproportionate emphasis on regulations and rituals at the expense of the relationships with and needs of their children. These regulations and rituals are sometimes grafted into the parents' minds via membership in a church, religious ideology, or some other group that is bent toward fanaticism, which can be the cause of this type of parenting. Many times, internal emotional conflicts or conflicts between adults in a home can be the cause of stringent, harsh and inflexible parenting models.

Regardless of where one may find himself/herself on a continuum of being parented or parenting, effort can always be made to correct or improve oneself. There is a myriad of sources for this improvement. There is group therapy, individual counseling (or therapy), family therapy (or counseling), support groups, (which ironically enough are often found in the best church communities), other types of groups that offer support of one type or other, good mentoring, great role modeling, many self-help books, quality sermons and lectures, many classes at colleges and universities, even degree programs, are only some of the ways that one can find the path to healing their brokenness. In point of fact, one can actually learn to parent him/herself. So all is not lost by any means.

Somehow, someway, I missed the boat and ended up broken, impulsive and misguided around my adult romantic connections. I chose badly quite often and I myself was not the best choice. It may have something to do with growing up with a very intense and neurotic grannie, (albeit sweet and loving in her own way) in the absence of both parents - a geographically long way from either of them. It may also have to do with losing my virginity to a considerably older woman who had even more unfulfilled needs than I, just as I was getting out of high school.

Because of my own inadequacies and brokenness, I found myself in a very toxic romantic relationship after a failed marriage. I looked to romance to heal old wounds that were left raw and untreated. It was the worst thing that I could have done, or anyone can do for that matter. The best Rorschach (an inkblot test that is used in psychiatry/psychology to help determine the nature or type of one's mental or psychological diagnoses) one will find to evaluate one's own brokenness, emotional insecurity, indiscipline and immaturity as well as the quality of the manner in which one was parented, is to foray into an adult romantic relationship. To the keen or even casual observer, it will reveal many of the deficiencies in one's psyche. You will see it in your partner as well as yourself, if you are paying attention and not too defensive or deeply wrapped in a garb of denial and self-deception. I saw lots of stuff in me. I was way too needy and broken…..without even being aware of it. My partner, while focusing her lens on my stuff, completely it seemed, missed all of her warts and blemishes. Jesus Christ, my Hero, who's allowed me true redemption, famously said, (my paraphrase), "why search for the speck in your brother's eye my sister, when you have to negotiate the plank or boulder in your own eye to find his."

Toxic relationships - at least some - are those filled with narcissism, hidden agendas, arrogance and an unwillingness to take responsibility for one's demons or one's pathology. The toxicity plays out in emotional dependency (instead of emotional inter-dependency), betrayal, cheating, vindictive reactions to hurt, dysfunctional communication patterns and over-sexualized attachments, to name just a few. My relationship broke off with my partner, painting me as a demon for my cheating and the lies told to try to cover that behavior up. She blazed a trail of betrayed confidences, distorted and ugly characterizations and allegations passed off as the gospel truth, to which she swore allegiance. Lucky for her, there was an audience more than happy to drink it all in. This only increased her power and strength with them.

They cheered as she was finally able to have the strength to leave the devil behind her.

The path to healing and "true love" is inextricably bound to humility, self-awareness, and a deep search for non-toxic connections, i.e. meaningful platonic relationships with the same and opposite sex, and a willingness to "do the work" which often involve sacrifice and pain but will ultimately result in fulfillment, peace and growth.

As noted above, there are many ways one can find support in their path to healing. Along with short periods of psychotherapy, I stumbled upon B6, under an umbrella organization known as "108". Troy, the Group's Founder, some 9 years ago now, through his own spiritual and psychological journey of healing and growth, met me broken and knew instantly I needed his shop. Much of the time, groups that are imbalanced (or homogeneous), like all men or all women, all boys, or all girls, all christians, all gays or lesbians, can have unintended effects, such as being too pro a cause and anti another. Some of these groups end up bashing the very thing that they came together to create in the first place, which are generally speaking, more harmonious and healthy outcomes in relationships. Some of these groups, either informally sitting around in a social setting or more formally convened, will inadvertently betray the very principles that brought them together. B6 is different. Its members are challenged every week to become more self-aware, take responsibility for their own messes in their lives and humbly yield their own narrow views of themselves to the more objective scrutiny of a "community".

The hurt that I experienced from the guilt, shame, rejection, ostracism, even persecution from that particular relationship, became fuel for the long and painful journey ahead toward growth and healing. B6 provided the necessary shelter during this wintry season of my life. Guys came together every week, under the auspicious and committed, not to mention very capable leadership of Troy Jones, to examine themselves through thoughtful and provocative discussions on a variety of relevant topics. During this time I never missed a session. It was nourishing food for the soul. While bawling inside week to week, I found guys who were at various stages on their own journey. Some were truly broken and desperate, and some were struggling on different spiritual and psychological levels.

Serendipity took me to a beautiful poem by Mário de Andrade (Sao Paulo 1893 - 1945) - Poet, novelist, essayist, and musicologist. He was one of the founders of Brazilian modernism. This poem sums it all up for me in terms of where I find myself now on my healing path - still broken and still far too inadequate but with so much more awareness and a much stronger need to put pieces back together.

Here's the poem: [insertions italicized in bracket are my own]

MY SOUL IS IN A HURRY

"I counted my years and discovered that I now have less time left to live than I had lived until now.

I feel like the kid who won a pack of candy; He ate the first few with pleasure, [*with several cavities and even a few rotten teeth*], but when he realized there were few left, he began to savor them deeply.

I don't have time for endless meetings where we discuss bylaws, rules, procedures and internal regulations, knowing that nothing will happen.

I no longer have time to put up with absurd people who, despite their chronological age, have not grown up.

My time is too short to discuss titles. I want the essential, my soul is in a hurry...

Without many sweets in the package...

I want to live next to human people, very human. Who know how to laugh at their mistakes, who are not vain of their triumphs. People who don't consider themselves elected before their time, people who don't try to escape their responsibilities. I am looking for people who defend human dignity, people who only want to walk on the side of truth and honesty [*not their own convenient truth*].

The essential is what makes life worth living.

I want to surround myself with people who know how to touch people's hearts...

People who have learned from the hard knocks of life to grow up with soft touches in their soul

Yes..., I am in a hurry..., I am in a hurry to live with the intensity that only maturity can give.

I intend not to waste any of the candy I have left... [*with repaired teeth and far healthier gums*] I am sure they will be more exquisite than the ones I have eaten so far.

My goal is to arrive at the end satisfied and at peace with my loved ones and with my conscience.

We have two lives and the second one starts when you realize that you have only one......"

I want the same things that Andrade wants. In addition, I would like to enjoy my remaining candy, next to and shared with another soul that I wouldn't hurt as I have so many before, while enjoying some of theirs without the pain from their brokenness. Friendship recession can logically lead to intimacy recession and in some cases, even depression. Transparency and authenticity are important pathways to both - deep friendships and fulfilling intimacy. Doing the work is the highway to getting there.

AUTHOR'S NOTE

Dear Readers,

As we come to the end of "Real Men are Sexier When They are Transparent," I am filled with a profound sense of gratitude and reflection. This journey, years in the making, has been a testament to the power of vulnerability, resilience, and connection.

From the inception of our stories to the final pages of this book, we've encountered numerous challenges. Many men who wanted to share their truths hesitated, held back by social norms, fear of judgment, and the weight of past traumas. It's a sobering realization that often, the fear of dishonoring those who hurt us outweighs the courage to heal ourselves. Yet, despite these obstacles, we persisted.

To my fellow authors, I extend my deepest appreciation for your unwavering commitment to transparency. Your courage to confront societal norms and share your vulnerabilities has been both inspiring and transformative. Together, we've shattered stereotypes, embraced vulnerability, and celebrated the transformative power of transparency.

To you, our cherished readers, I offer my heartfelt thanks. Your willingness to embark on this journey with us, to engage with our stories, and to reflect on your own experiences has been both humbling and inspiring. It is through your eyes that our words find meaning, and it is in your hearts that our stories find resonance.

As we close this chapter, I am thrilled to announce that this is just the beginning. We plan to continue producing additional volumes as long as men are willing to share their truths. Moreover, we are claiming the Friday before Father's Day as "Healthy Masculinity Day" to provide an additional opportunity to celebrate those men who show up every day but are often unseen.

Remember, dear readers that the journey to authenticity is not always easy, but it is always worth it. In the moments of doubt and uncertainty, may you find solace in the knowledge that you are not alone—that there are others, like us, who walk this path alongside you.

And so, as we bid farewell to these pages, let us carry with us the courage to be seen, the wisdom to listen, and the compassion to understand. For in the end, it is our shared humanity that binds us together, making us stronger, wiser, and infinitely more beautiful.

With deepest gratitude and warmest wishes,

Pastor Troy R. Jones and Author of "Real Men are Sexier When They are Transparent"

Made in the USA
Middletown, DE
06 January 2026

24407949R00055